"I Will Dance Again"

By Shane Bailey

ISBN 978-0-359-42684-3

The Delilah Mae Bailey Story

Table of contents….

"I Will Dance Again"

Who is Delilah Mae Bailey?

Delilah is almost 5 years old now, and goes to school at Hirsch Elementary in Spring, Texas. Curly blond hair and, blue eyes with an attitude of a million man army. She loves to sing, dance, skateboard, roller skate, ride her bike, fish, play football, basketball, and anything else she can get her little hands on.

Her favorite colors right now are pink and blue, her favorite number is 17, and she loves JoJo Siwa. Her favorite song is "twinkle little star",and says she is going to marry Mylo L. even if her daddy doesn't want her to .

Delilah is a ballerina and tap dancer at "The PAC" Performing Arts Center in Spring, TX now. She is now getting ready for her first recital in May of 2019, which she is very excited about.

Delilah had hip dysplasia at birth on both of her legs. The Amanda and, I were told by her pediatrician to double diaper her for a few months and she should be fine which we did. After about 11 or 12 months Delilah was cleared of hip dysplasia completely by her pediatrician. Little did we know her nightmare had only just began.

Who is Delilah Mae Bailey?

This is her story through the eyes of many that were by her side through it all. How our little girl could be so strong through some of her darkest hours and dance again.

Who is Delilah Mae Bailey?

Her big smile...

"The Bad News"

Delilah was very active, running around with her friends bossing them around, and tormenting her older brother Gage in the process. I took her fishing with me one day, and she hung a gigantic turtle. She tried her best to reel him in but then said "Daddy I'm Tired", and handed me the rod and reel.

When she was about 2 and a half years old my wife, and I started noticing her wobble when she walked. We were both curious so we asked the pediatrician to x-ray her legs again. The pediatrician immediately said "get her to a surgeon as soon as possible".

We took her to U.T Hospital in downtown Houston to be x-rayed again. The surgeon that reviewed the x-rays was baffled that the pediatrician did not catch this in the follow up visits we had with them. She pointed out how far her legs were out of socket.

We then took her to Texas Children's Hospital in downtown Houston for one more x-ray. They were also baffled that the pediatrician could possibly over look something so obvious. I remember when the doctor came in to tell us the news of the x-rays.

"The Bad News"

"The Bad News"

I'm not sure if it was butterflies, anger, or sadness when we heard the news of what our little girl would soon have to go through because of some ones mistake. We were told Delilah would have to have three surgeries, and would not be able to walk, and they didn't even want her to move if possible.

My wife and I were both upset, knowing changes for all of us were coming sooner than we could have ever imaged.

To give you a little insight into what hip dysplasia is, here you go. Hip dysplasia occurs when the femur ball of the leg is out of the hip socket. The leg is dislocated and does not develop normally.

Hip dysplasia is a condition typically present at birth. The hip doesn't work properly, and worsens without correction.

There are several different types of hip dysplasia. Acetabular dysplasia, subluxable, subluxed, dislocatable, and dislocated.

Hip dysplasia seems to run in families. In addition, being in the breech position sometimes puts stress on the baby's hip and thigh muscles, causing a hip to move out of the joint.

Hip dysplasia occurs in approximately one in 1,000 births.

The earlier hip dysplasia is discovered and treated, the greater your child's chances for a successful correction. Hip dysplasia might prevent or delay milestones, such as sitting and crawling. If left untreated, hip dysplasia can lead to walking abnormalities, a limb length difference, early arthritis or hip pain.

"Delilah's Diagnosis"

Delilah had severe hip dysplasia at birth. Both legs were completely dislocated, due to breach and Amanda had to have a c-section.

We were told to double diaper her for a little over a year, by her pediatrician. She was soon cleared of hip dysplasia.

We would later find out, the double diapering never worked. Her legs were still completely dislocated, and it was apparent someone did not know how to read an x-ray.

She should have been put in a pelvic harness, it has a very high correction rate.

The pelvic harness has a 90% chance of correction rate using it at an early age.

Her devil horn hair do.

It's hard to believe how strong she is.

"Before Surgery"

Delilah Mae Bailey was born March 6, 2014 at Memorial Herman Hospital in the Woodlands TX.

Holding Delilah for the first time changed my life forever. She was beautiful just like her mother. It took me a while to get used to being a parent, but It all worked out ok. Holding her in my arms, and singing her songs to put her to sleep will always be there in my heart when I think of my little girl.

Like any father should be, I am very protective of my daughter. When she first learned to crawl, I was just a little paranoid, but walk, and run kind of threw me over the edge.

"Before Surgery"

At birth we were informed she had hip dysplasia in both legs. I had no clue on exactly what hip dysplasia was. I wasn't sure on anything or how serious it was. The pediatrician informed us she would need to be double diapered for a few months. After checkup after checkup she was finally cleared after about a year.

My wife and I were so happy it was all over. It took a while to get used to only putting one diaper on her. Delilah learned to walk and was potty-trained shortly after. She loved it. She started saying she is not a baby she a big girl, and wanted to do everything herself, and she did. She was happy and so were we.

"Before Surgery"

"Before Surgery"

Delilah was always a strong little girl from birth, never letting anyone tell her what to do besides us, which she fought them when she heard the word no. We would get out in the yard, and play tag or football normally, but if I made a touch down or tagged her out I was the cheater and she would quit.

Normally my wife, and I would cook up a bunch of food on the weekends, and invite our families and friends over. There were always lots and lots of kids. We normally would get a bounce house to keep them all occupied.

"Before Surgery"

Delilah loved the bounce house and, would normally yell at the bigger kids for bouncing too much in it. "Take off your shoes" "Quit jumping so high" "I'm going to tell my momma" "I'm going to tell my daddy". The list goes on and on.

We had to take Delilah for Pre-Op for her first surgery in October 2016. We were highly stressed during the drive up to Texas Children's Hospital. It was just Pre-Op but it was getting closer, and closer to her first of many surgeries.

"Before Surgery"

"Before Surgery"

We put together a massive list of questions for pre op to ask the doctor about. Could she fit in a car seat with the cast? Doctor's answer: No. Will she be able to fit in her stroller? Doctor's answer: No, She will have a wheel chair.

We asked if she would be able to walk, or crawl at all. Doctor's answer: No, I don't want her moving at all. Can we give her a bath? Doctor's answer: No, just wipe her down with a sponge. Do not get the cast wet at all.

How will she be put to sleep before surgery? Doctor's answer: Anesthesia. The doctor gave her a few options, bubble gum, strawberry, cherry, banana, or grape. Delilah said she wanted bubble gum.

"Before Surgery"

"Before Surgery"

Sitting in the waiting room, waiting for Delilah to be called back, seemed like it took a life time. Good thing Texas Children's Hospital had plenty of toys, and kids to play with. Delilah found her a play house to hang out in while we waited and she was happy.

When they finally called her back to check her heart rate, height, and weight she was very upset to leave all her new friends she had met while waiting. From there they took us down stairs to another waiting room which we would sit there for about another hour before speaking to anyone.

While we sat, Delilah was getting angry because this waiting room had no toys, or kids to play with. Delilah had to get blood work done before her first surgery in November of 2016 so we just waited and waited some more.

Finally a doctor, a nurse, or physician of some type came out to get Delilah for blood work. Delilah was scared but followed them into another room.

She came back out a few minutes later crying, and ran straight to me. Holding her in my arms while she was crying brought anger into my heart, because of a mistake made by someone who is fully trained, and gets paid to correct this type of diagnoses at an early stage.

They told us at birth she had hip dysplasia. They told us to double diaper and we did. They told us she was clear of hip dysplasia when she never was.

"Before Surgery"

"Before Surgery"

On our way home, Amanda, and I decided to throw Delilah a party before her surgeries started, and she could not walk. We rented a bounce house, and let her pick out the banner she wanted on it. She chose Minnie Mouse so that's what she got.

We rented a large tent, Lots of tables and chairs, cooked hamburgers and hot dogs on the grill. We invited everyone that had a kid to come over, and play with her before it all started. Only a hand full showed up but she still had fun.

I remember watching her that day, running, jumping and all over the place. She had the biggest smile on her face, which was all we wanted as parents. It was hard not to think of what was to come.

She didn't realize what was about to happen. I think that day Amanda and I covered up our true emotions to make sure our little girl kept smiling.

"Before Surgery"

"Before Surgery"

Delilah was nervous, but was still running around playing with toys while we waited for the doctor to come get her for surgery. We were both stressed out, but tried our best to stay calm.

As we were watching Delilah play, the surgeon's showed up with a toy police car for her to ride in down to the surgery room. Once she was loaded up, we both gave her a big hug and kiss then they wheeled her away down a long narrow hallway.

She looked back one last time at us, and then the wooden double doors shut. We watched her through the window of the double doors until she faded in the distance of the hallway.

We were told by the doctor the surgery would last a few hours, and they would call us when she was in the recovery room.

"Before Surgery"

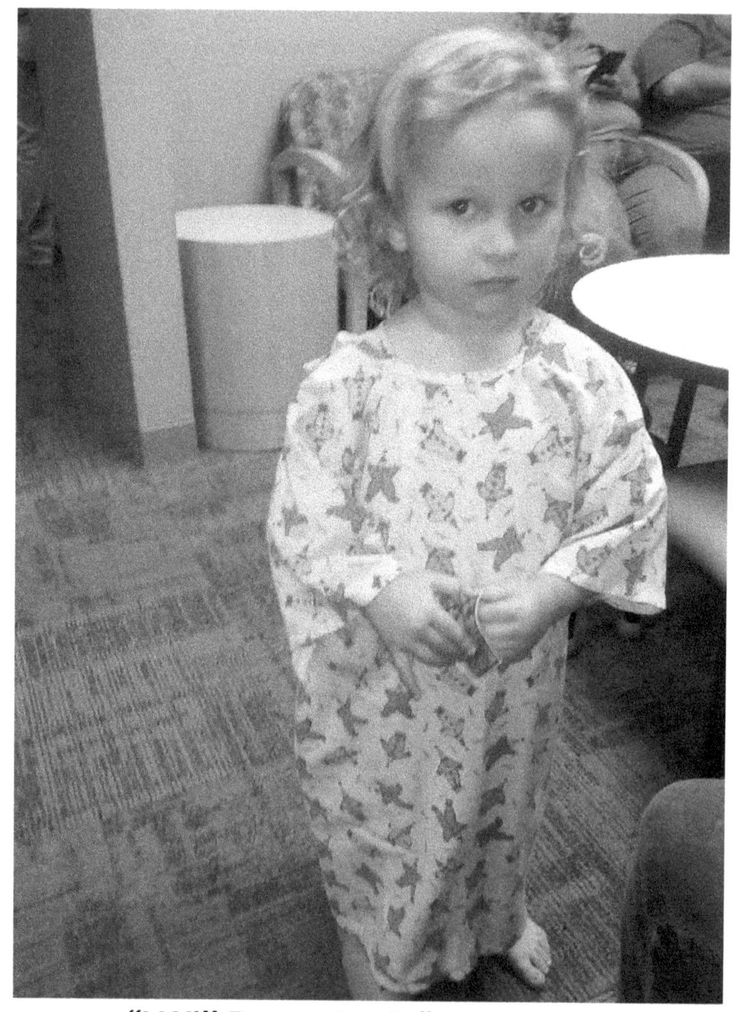

"The Surgery"

Walking around waiting on her surgery to be over, felt like a life time. Amanda's parents, Len and Gail, took us to a Mexican restaurant, about a mile down the road, to kill a little time. It was nice to get out of the hospital for a little while.

We still couldn't take our minds off of our little girl in surgery. We were both worried and didn't know what to expect when we got the phone call from the doctor.

"The Surgery"

The doctor finally called, and said Delilah was being moved to the recovery room, and we could come see her. We hurried back to the hospital and, walked into the recovery room.

As we walked down the hallway, and into the room sadness started creeping in. We finally saw her off to the left of the recovery room. She was still asleep from anesthesia.

Amanda, and I both, were in a state of shock at that point. Delilah was wrapped in blankets, and hooked to all sorts of machines.

We both tried our best to hold back the tears, and remember lots of kids have been in the same situation as Delilah. Well, that didn't work, we both started crying our eyes out.

"The Surgery"

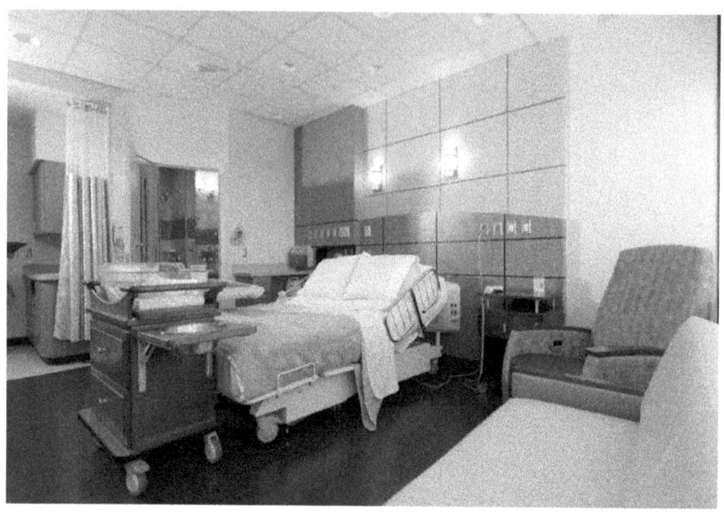

After we calmed down a little, Amanda pulled back the blankets to see the cast on her legs. Then we were back to crying again.

She had a pink cast that wrapped around her waist, her complete right leg, and half way down her left leg with a bar attaching both legs to keep her legs spread out in a certain position.

"Before Surgery"

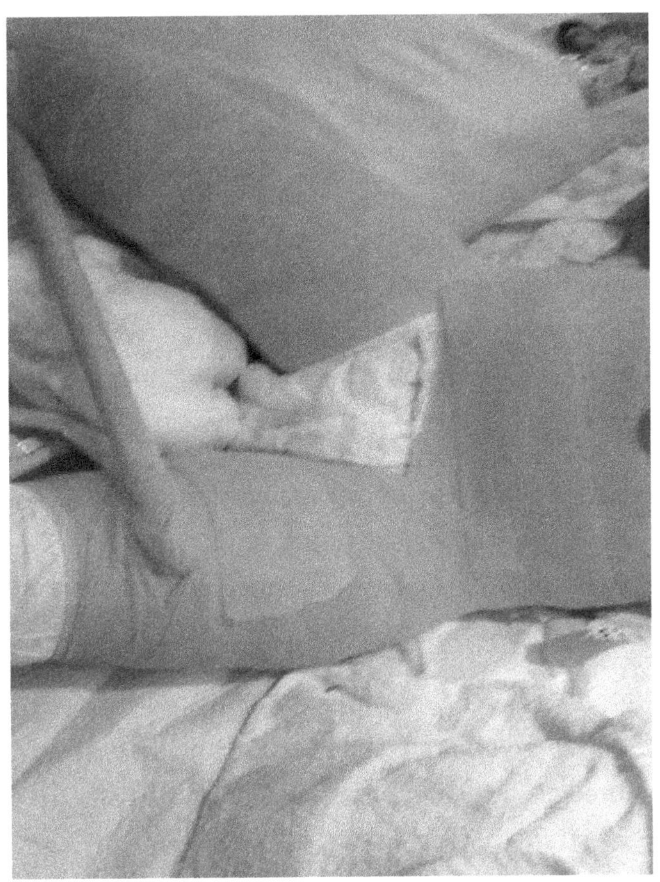

As parents we were stunned. We started thinking about how we would deal with everyday life, now that she was in a cast. Can we pick her up? Will it hurt her? Can we hold her?

There were so many question marks bouncing around in our heads at that moment. After about an hour or, two Delilah finally started to wake up. She was very confused, on where she was, and why she could not move.

As the pain medications from anesthesia started wearing off, she started screaming, and crying. The nurses came over, and gave her some liquid valium through her IV.

She started screaming even more, and her whole body started turning blood red. We called the nurse back over immediately to check her out. Delilah had an allergic reaction to the valium.

The nurses then gave her something else through her IV, and the redness started to slowly fade away. She finally calmed down, after a while and went back to sleep.

Hours, and hours later the hospital finally had a room for Delilah available. It had been a very long day for our little girl. When she woke up again, the nurses released her to go to her room.

We were so happy just to be able to sit down, and hold our daughters little hand. They wheeled her bed down to the elevators and up to the room.

We were all exhausted and ready for bed when we got there, but little did we know night shift had just begun.

"Before Surgery"

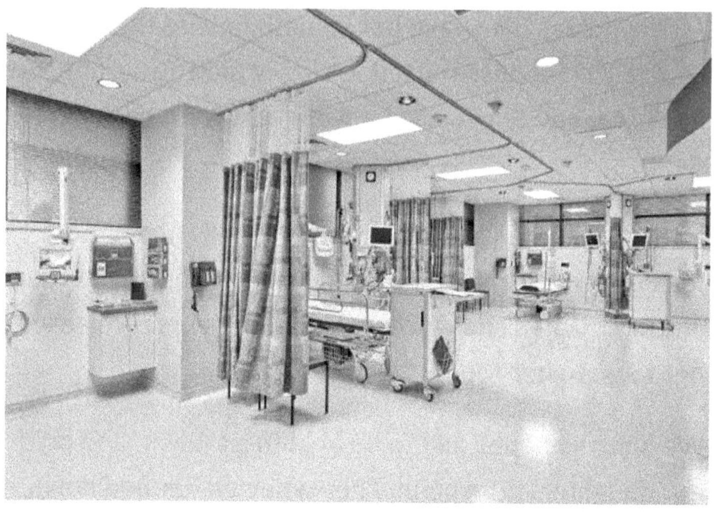

Delilah was still a sleep, so we laid on the couch next to her, to try to close our eyes for a little while. A few minutes later Delilah started regurgitating and could not breathe. We quickly hit the page button on Delilah's bed, to get the nurses in there to help.

We held her head up so she would spit out what was coming up and could breathe. I walked into the hallway to try to flag down a nurse. With no one in sight, we were starting to get angry.

The nurses finally showed up a few minutes later to get Delilah changed and calmed back down. As we watched the clock on the wall slowly ticking away, we knew then we could not sleep.

One of us would stay awake for a few hours, just holding onto her precious little hand, while the other would sleep.

Dawn arrived within a blink of an eye, and Delilah was awake. She was starting to realize her ability to walk, and move around had been taken from her.

She was very depressed and it showed. There was no smile on this beautiful little girls face. Nothing to look forward to, and nothing to do besides watch cartoons on T.V.

The nurses came back in to get her early that morning for an MRI. Delilah looked at me, and said "I want to go home daddy" as we went down a couple of floors in the elevator to the MRI room.

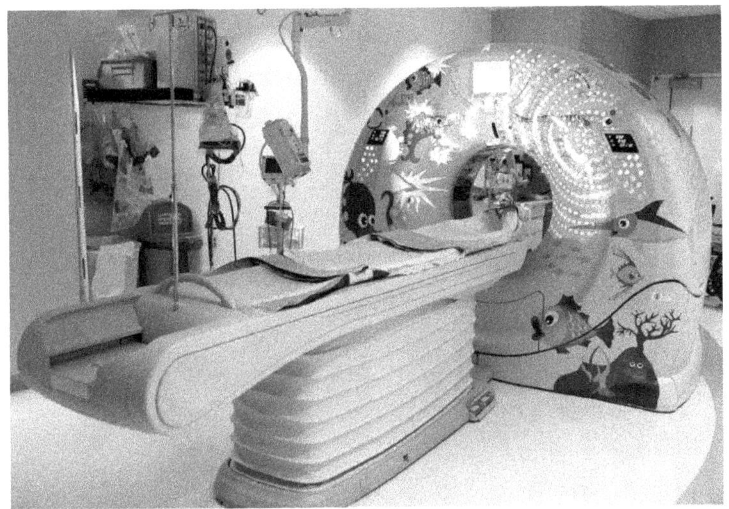

Delilah was scared, because the machine made loud banging noises while she was inside of it. I held her hand to comfort her while they were taking the pictures.

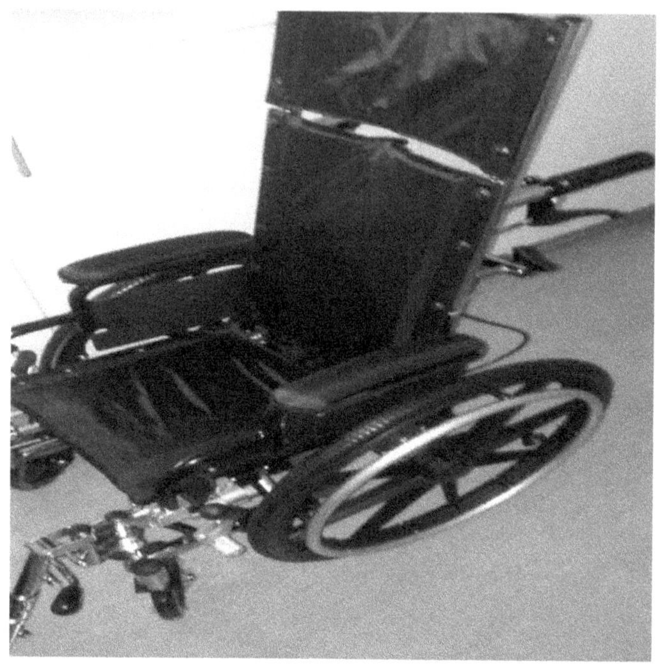

When we finally made it back to the room exhausted, after another couple hours of testing. A few minutes later the wheel chair company arrived with Delilah's chair.

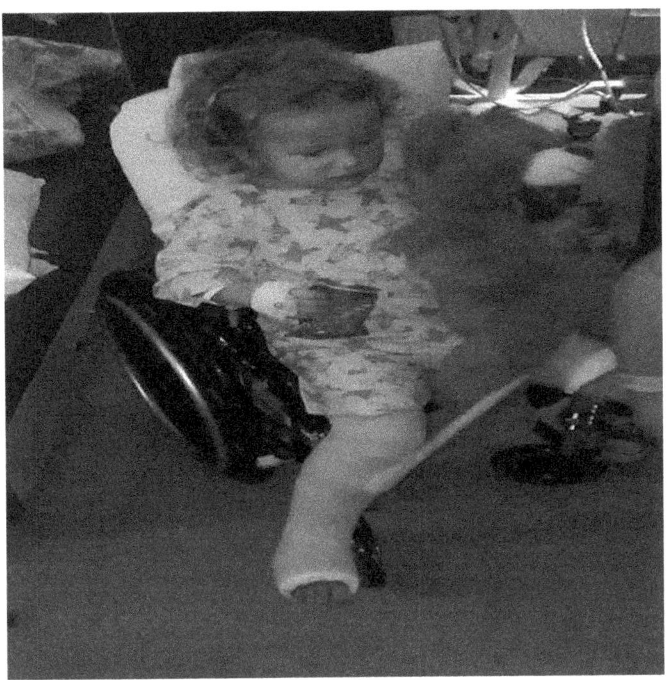

She was still sad, but at least we could take her on trips around the hospital. It took us a little while with a little help from the doctors, and nurses to get her in the chair without hurting her.

Delilah hated the fact she could not walk. You could see it in her eyes. I think she was a little excited just to be outside though.

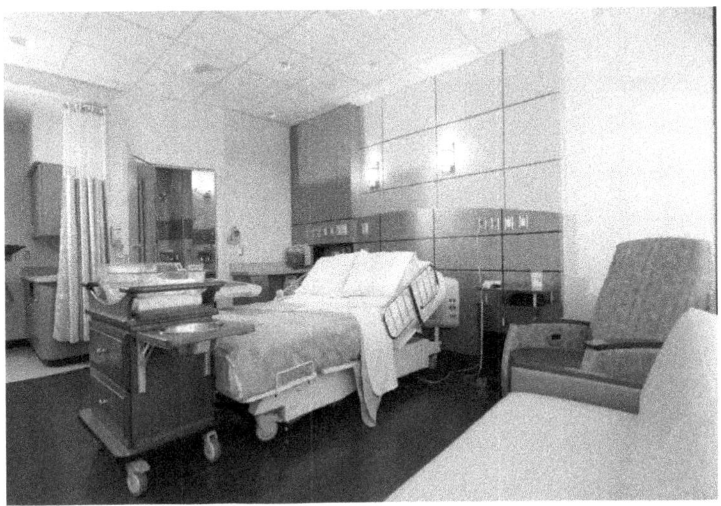

We got back to the room, after a short stroll around the hospital and just relaxed for a little while. Shortly after, we heard a knock on the door.

It was Delilah's best friends Mylo and, Jasper. Delilah was so excited to see them.

"The Hospital Stay"

The next day Delilah got to see Santa Clause. That's a very good thing about having your kid at Texas Children's Hospital. They try their best to keep kids smiling.

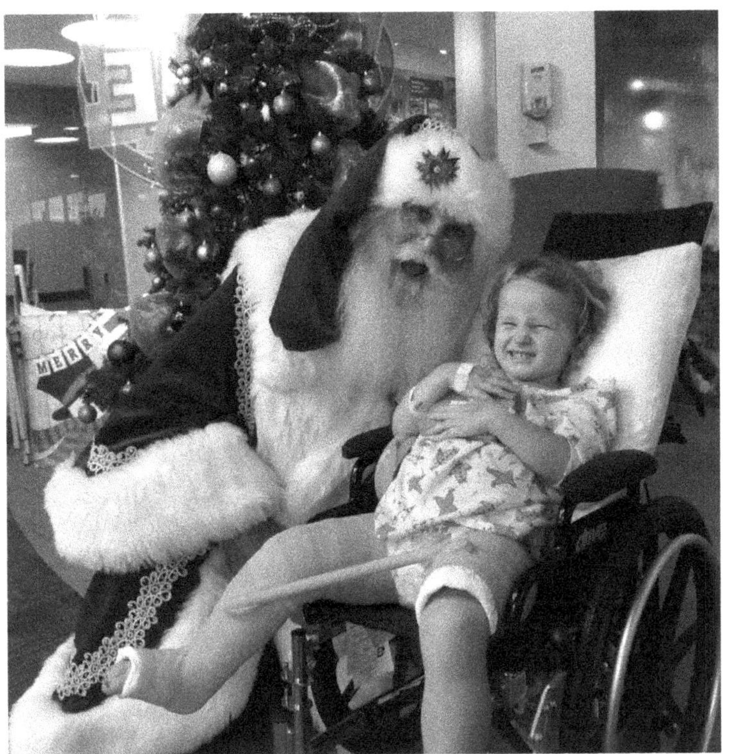

Delilah tried hard to smile big for Santa.

She loves getting gifts from Santa.

"The Hospital Stay"

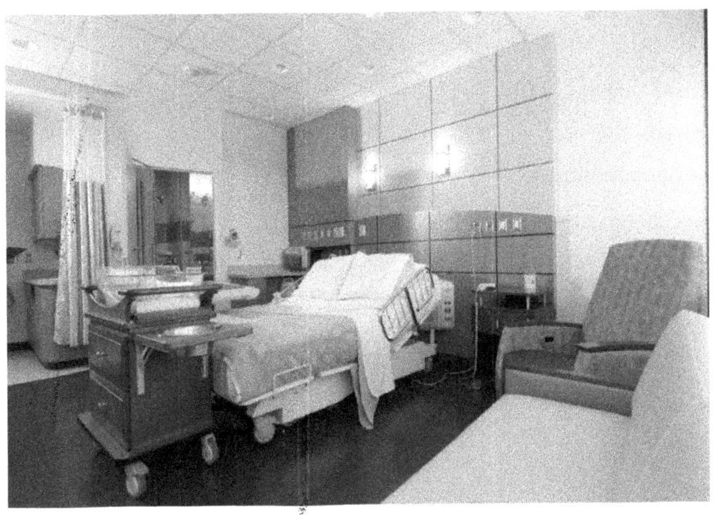

Delilah had quite a few visitors, while she was at the hospital. She was happy they came to see her. She told her little friends, she could not walk because the doctor took her walking legs away.

It's funny how kids think. It's the little things that will keep you going in your hardest times in life. It's the little things that will count in the end.

"She's coming home"

Delilah hated being at the hospital, constrained to a bed, or a wheel chair but, she still found reasons to smile. After a few long days at the hospital, it was finally release day.

We were all so eager to go home. Just tired and, worn down. We told Delilah she was going to get to go home today. She was so happy.

"She's coming home"

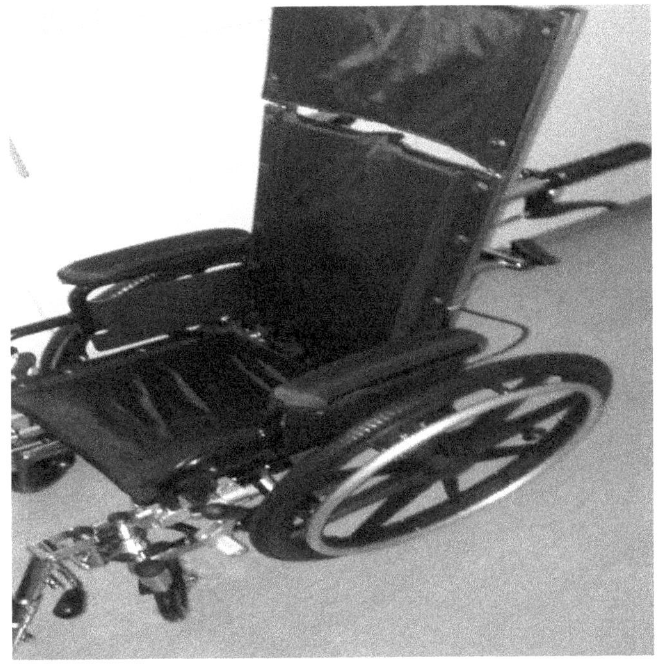

We were told by the hospital, she would be released early that morning. We waited and waited some more. Finally a few hours later the doctors came in to release her.

We signed the paper work and packed up to go. The nurses helped put Delilah in the wheel chair, and then we were off. Down the elevator, through the hall, pass the lobby, out the double glass doors.

"She's coming home"

The valet driver immediately showed up with our car. We had to carefully lay Delilah into the back seat of the car without hurting her.

It was a hard task, but I think we managed it o.k. We folded up the wheel chair and, crammed it into the trunk along with the rest of our things.

"She's coming home"

Delilah was so happy to be on her way home. She looked very uncomfortable, and wanted to set up in her seat to see how close she was but, couldn't.

She smiled though, and tried her best to see anything that reminded her of home.

We finally turned into our neighborhood, and made it to our driveway. We popped the trunk, and unloaded the wheel chair. We got it set up, and placed Delilah in it.

She looked around and smiled so big. She knew she was home. As we unloaded the rest of our stuff from the car, Delilah looked down the road to see her friends running and playing. She screamed out, and waved to draw their attention.

Her little friends waved back, and came running toward her. Delilah was talking their heads off even before they got to her. Her friends asked her if she could come play with them down the street.

Delilah responded: I can't, the doctor took my walking legs. She wanted to go play so bad. She looked at us with tears in her eyes but, she knew she couldn't go. Her friends shortly left to go back down the street to play.

Delilah was heartbroken. She stared off in the distance as her little friends walked further, and further away. With tears in her eyes, and all hope in her heart lost at that moment, she still tried her best to smile.

As we wheeled Delilah into the house, she kept looking back in the distance to see if her friends were coming back. They never did.

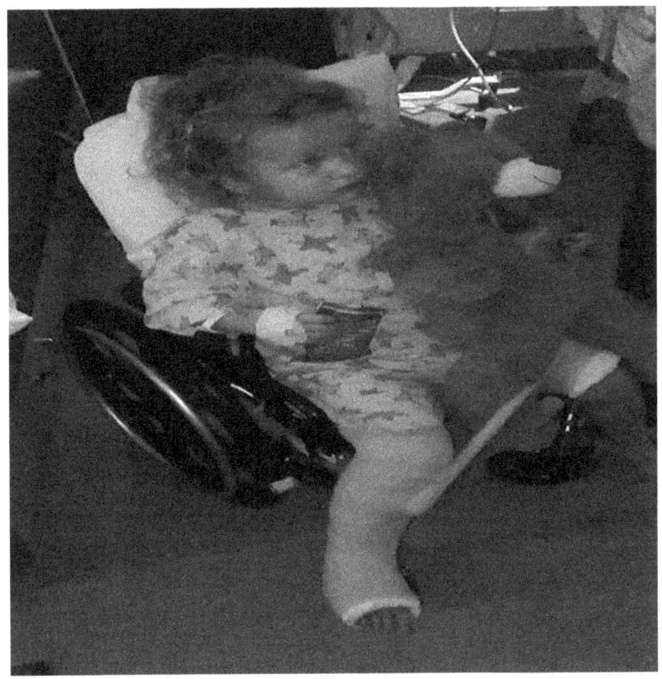

I understand kids will be kids, and love to play but, seeing the expression Delilah had on her face that day as we brought her in broke our hearts. I think what hurt the most was not being able to do anything about it.

She couldn't do much at all. No more dancing, running around with her friends, she just sat in her wheel chair watching cartoons and, wishing she could go walking around with her friends.

The first couple of weeks were long and, hard. She was in a lot of pain and depressed. Trying to move her around without hurting her was a challenge.

Something simple as changing a diaper turned into an obstacle course. It was harder than we ever thought it would be and really scary.

One day some of Delilah's grandparents stopped by to hang out with her for the day. Delilah told her grandma she wanted to walk on the grass again, because it was soft. Grandma replied: You will soon enough.

Delilah then said she missed the sweet smell of flowers on the ground. Grandma then, pulled up a flower, and gave it to her.

Delilah smiled, and said the flower smells so good. Grandma then asked Delilah if she wanted to dance. Delilah responded: I can't, my legs don't work anymore.

Grandma responded: Yes you can, I'll show you how. Delilah smiled, and asked how. Grandma wheeled her into the garage where music was being played.

She twirled Delilah around and around from one side of the room to the next. Delilah moved her head, and arms to the sound of the music.

Delilah was happy as she danced on through the song with her grandma. It seemed as a new spark of hope was shining through her.

That day she gained some hope. That day she realized there was nothing that could control the things she wanted to do in life.

It was simply up to her. Would she give up? Would she keep fighting back against this curse she had endured?

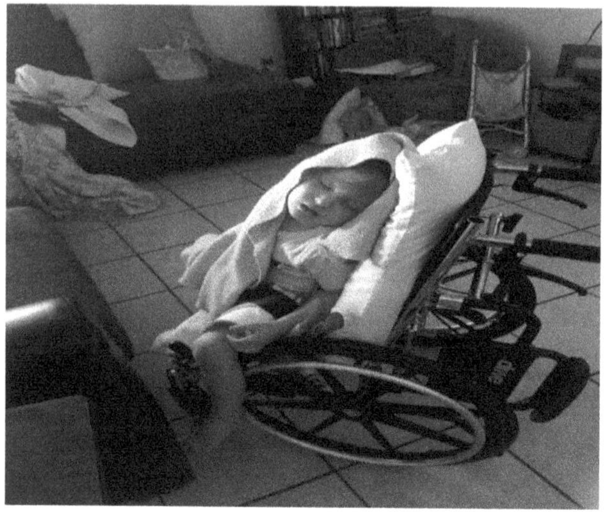

Delilah had a long road ahead of her, but only grew stronger each day. She started popping wheelies with her wheel chair, and chasing kids around the house.

Delilah said she's not night, night after a long day of rolling around in her chair.

Happy 3rd
Birthday
Delilah
Mae

Delilah loves her grandparents, as most kids do. They always spoil her with random acts of ice cream and candy. They were always there to cheer her up when she was down.

Delilah, with the support of many was slowly but, surely starting to get stronger. It took a while to get used of all the new complications she had but, she stood strong.

"The Second Surgery"

After twelve weeks in her cast, it was time to go back to Texas Children's Hospital. Delilah was glad to be getting the cast off her right leg but, didn't realize she was about to go through the whole process again with her left leg.

We tried to convince her she was almost half way through with all her surgery's to cheer her up a little.

"The Second Surgery"

Once again, she would be wheeled down that long fading hallway, once again she would disappear into the distance of bright lights, and she would look back one last time.

Hours went by as we waited to see her in the recovery room. Delilah picked out the color purple for the cast wrapping.

We finally got the call a few hours later and, hurried down to the recovery room to see her. We were a whole lot more prepared emotionally than her first surgery. We knew what to expect, and we knew our little girl was strong.

Nurses asked her what type of Popsicle she wanted, and gave her a few options, Strawberry, cherry, banana, or rainbow. Delilah chose rainbow of course. Just sitting in the recovery room I think she had about ten or fifteen of those popsicles. Might as well, she had a long wait for a room.

I think in a way, Delilah was in Popsicle heaven. She couldn't eat anything else, so why not? Between all the medications, the nurses were giving her, and the massive Popsicle intake, Delilah was really feeling good.

She was laughing, and joking around being goofy. We were so happy to see her gaining strength in a storm that just would not end.

"The Second Surgery"

"The Second Surgery"

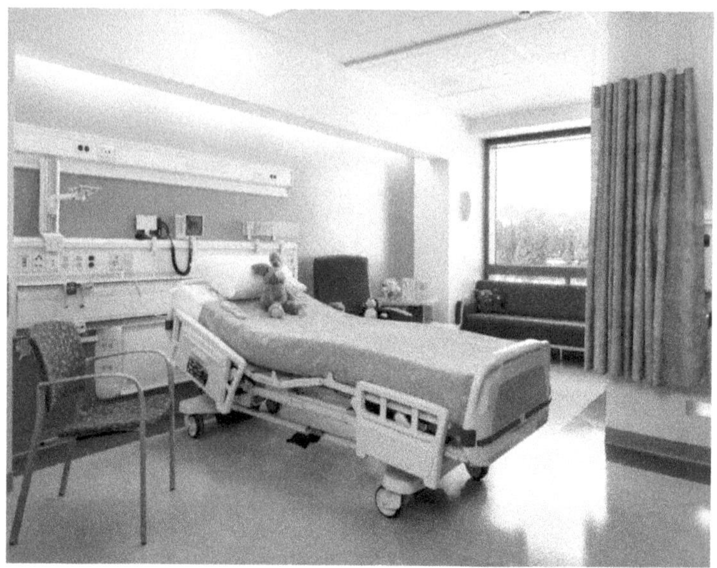

Delilah was so tired of being in the hospital, and not being able to walk. She looked so worn down, and depressed after her medications wore off.

Looking into her eyes you could see a question. She never came out, and asked it but I think it would have been something like this. Will I walk again?

"The Second Surgery"

A few days later, after many more test, Delilah was released from the hospital. Another cast but, same issues as before. Amanda and I were just tired of the situation.

The days past slowly, and the nights seem to never end. The days blended together to make one long one. We pleaded to god to just give us a sign this was all most over as we could see her starting to break.

All of our mental states were blown, but we knew we had to stay as strong as possible for her. Trying to function, felt like a one thousand pound weight tied to your legs and, no matter how hard you tried it still had the better of you.

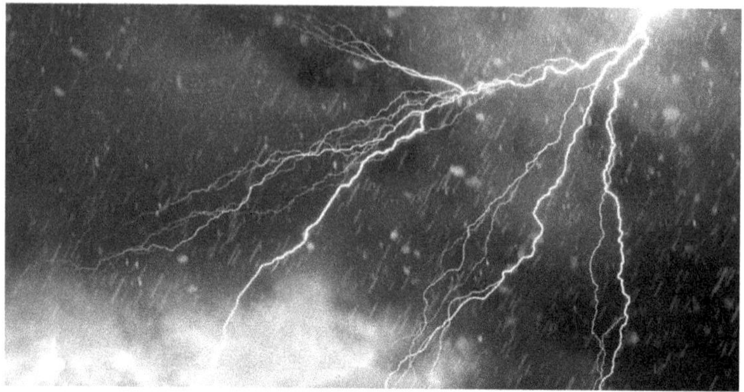

So the storm rolled on, and on not giving in for a second. Smiles were replaced with tears as time dragged on. Sanity was trying to walk out the door, as bad thoughts walked through our minds.

Luckily for me I had a random phone call from an old friend. He talked me down from doing something stupid that day. Not sure if he realized it, or not but it meant a lot to me that day. Thanks Jay Mansell.

That simple phone call meant a lot to me and, my family.

"The Second Surgery"

As the rain began to let up, and slowly wash away the clouds Delilah, although broken and torn kept going. It seems to me that you can stay strong for a while but, after a while it takes the life out of you.

Weeks went by, and it was finally time for the second cast off. Was it all over? No.

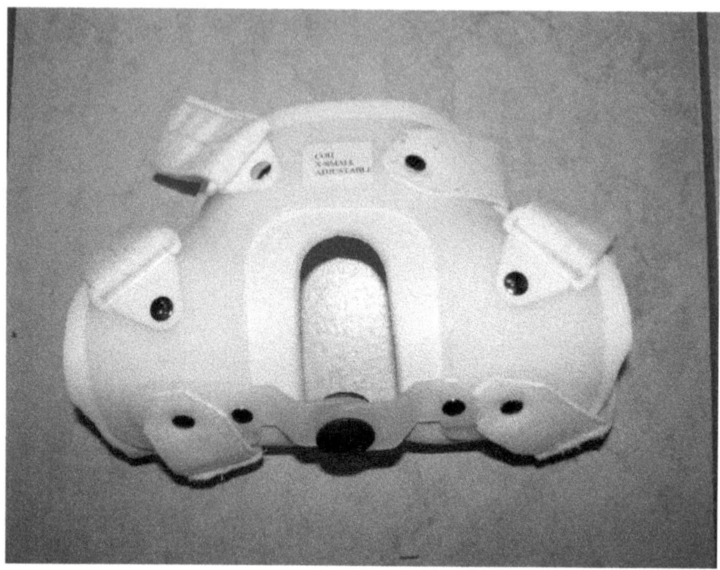

Delilah would then, be put a rhino brace for another 12 weeks. This thing was just another obstacle course to me. I'm sure some parents might think of it as simple, but not us.

Just look at this thing. Your child's legs are completely spread in an awkward position all the time. Trying to move her around, or even putting her in her wheel chair was difficult.

Delilah was getting used to all her complications, and soon enough it was time for physical therapy.

Finally the day came to get rid of the brace, and remove the screws. It only took a few hours, and she was in recovery. She screamed, and cried begging them to put the cast back on.

She was in a lot of pain. She still had to sleep with the rhino brace on, but did not wear it in the daytime. She could take full bathes at that point.

"Physical Therapy"

The road for Delilah was very long and hard. Picking her up out of that wheel chair to change her was terrible. Luckily I had all the right equipment to get the job done.

I don't miss this one bit but, I think Delilah enjoyed watching us suffer through it.

"Physical Therapy"

Learning to walk again was a challenge for her. We had to stretch her legs out a few times a day. She would scream and, cry. Twice a week for about a year, she went to a physical therapist to get her to stretch some more.

The first few months, she would drag herself around on the floor, afraid to use her legs. Soon enough, she started to pull herself up on to furniture, and walls to stand up. Her legs were shaky and weak. She was afraid to try to take any steps.

She finally took her first step soon after that. She was so happy. She had her walking legs back.

Once she took that first step, she got brave, and every step would need to be applauded. Every step she took was a milestone, and she would make sure everyone noticed.

She would scream out with excitement "I did it, I did it." "Did you see that?" "Watch This"

"Physical Therapy"

The storm slowly faded in the distance, and Delilah only grew stronger. She could walk again, she could run again, and now she would dance again.

"She's Dancing"

She fought hard to overcome a seemingly never ending storm. She held on to faith even when we lost ours. I'm proud to say she's our little girl. She said she would dance again and, she is.

"Ladies and gentlemen, please give a warm welcome to ballerina, Delilah Mae Bailey."

"She's Dancing"

"She's Dancing"

"She's Dancing"

"She's Dancing"

She loves her new friends.

One of her recital dresses.

"Delilah"

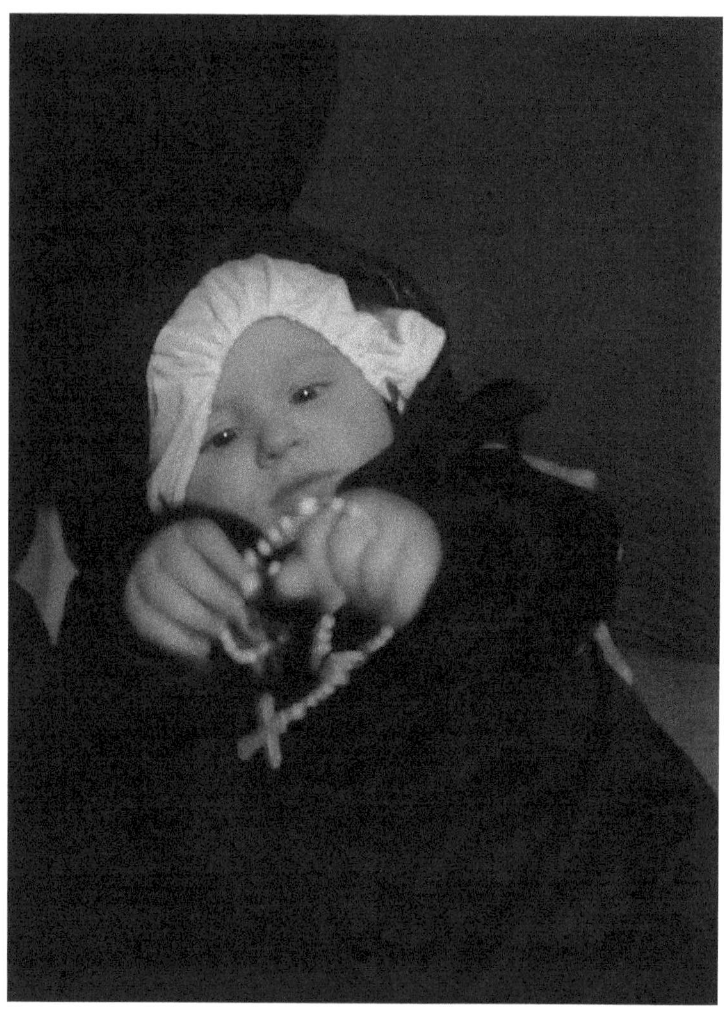

I always wanted Delilah to be a nun.

"Delilah"

Some of her ballerina friends.

"Delilah"

Tonight is Delilah's first Valentine's Day dance. I'm not sure who is more excited. Delilah looks beautiful as always and is as strong as ever. We recently found out, there will be another surgery on her left leg in the near future.

"Delilah"

"Delilah"

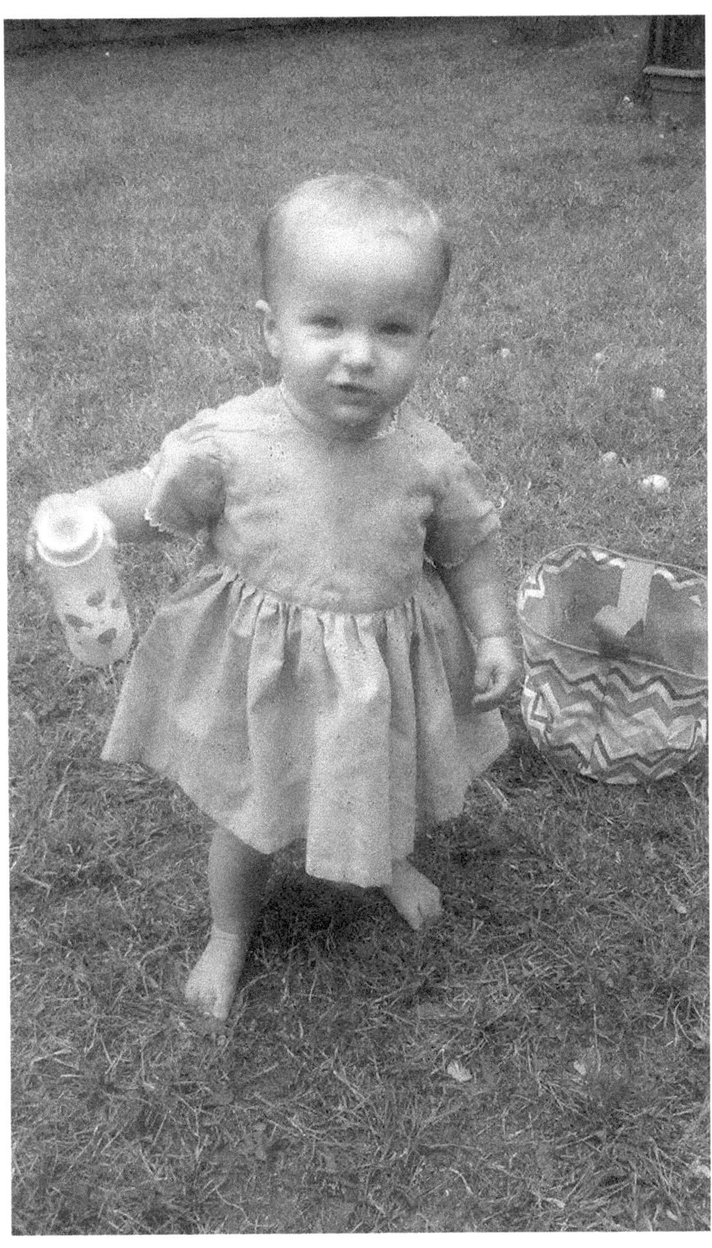

"Delilah"

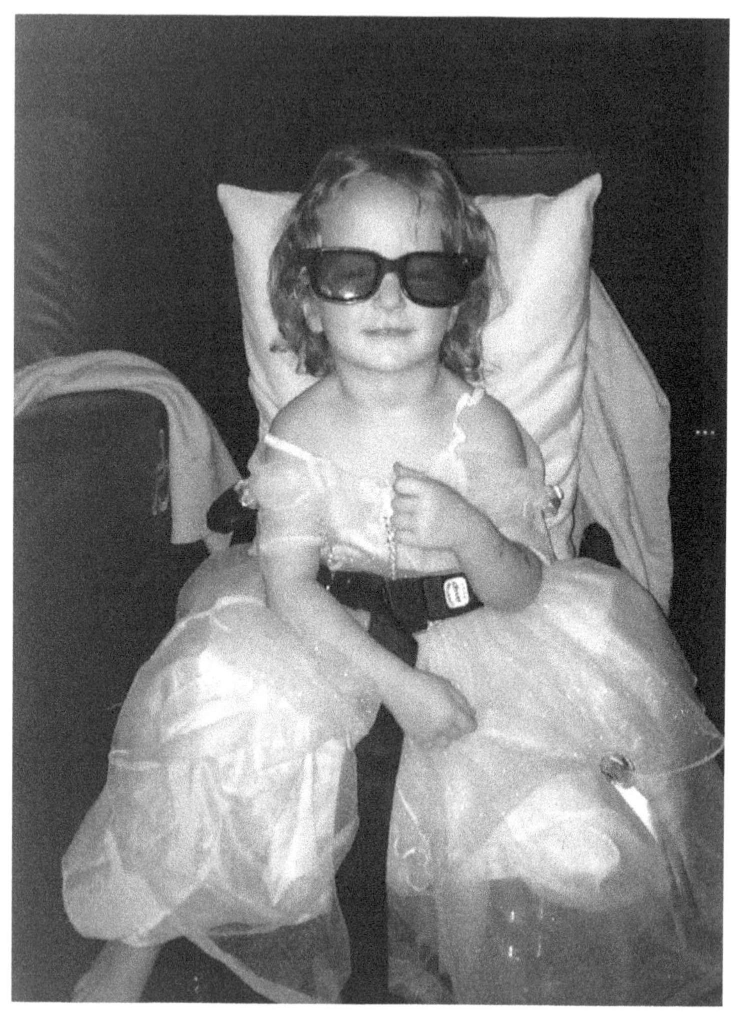

"Delilah"

"Delilah"

"Delilah"

"The Nut Cracker Band"

"Delilah"

"Delilah"

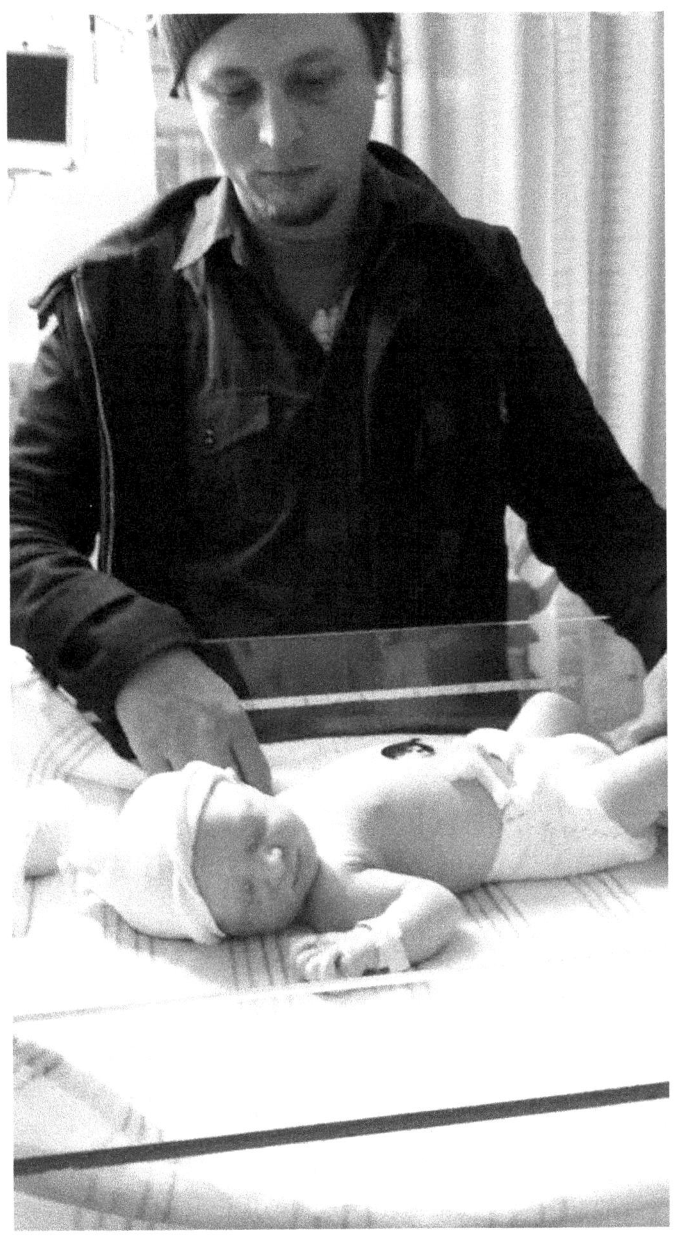

"Delilah"

"Delilah"

Our little nun.

"Delilah"

She loves to help clean and cook.

Halloween

"Delilah"

"Delilah"

Our little super heroes.

"Delilah"

"Delilah"

She's a real cowgirl.

"Delilah"

"In Loving Memory"

In loving memory of Len Bruso. We will always miss you. Time is short and very unpredictable. Have the boat ready when we get to the lake, I'll do the cooking. See you soon, we all love you.

www.ingramcontent.com/pod-product-compliance
Ingram Content Group UK Ltd.
Pitfield, Milton Keynes, MK11 3LW, UK
UKHW020241250726
13967UKWH00001B/489

9 780359 426843